PRACTICING THE BEATITUDES

Called to Be a Catechist

PRACTICING
the BEATITUDES

Inspiration and Professional Growth

TWENTY-THIRD PUBLICATIONS

twentythirdpublications.com

IMPRIMATUR

+ Most Reverend
  Robert J. McManus, STD,
  Bishop of Worcester,
  February 23, 2018

TWENTY-THIRD PUBLICATIONS
One Montauk Avenue, Suite 200, New London, CT 06320
(860) 437-3012 » (800) 321-0411 » www.twentythirdpublications.com

Cover photo: © shutterstock / Monkey Business Images

ISBN: 978-1-62785-295-1
Library of Congress Catalog Card Number: 2017941578
Printed in the U.S.A.

 A division of Bayard, Inc.

CONTENTS

INTRODUCTION 1

CHAPTER 1
The Beatitudes: Our Moral Compass. 3
David Wheeler-Reed

CHAPTER 2
The Foundation for Living the Beatitudes 10
Sean Reynolds

CHAPTER 3
Portrait and Promise of Discipleship 18
Susan K. Sack

CHAPTER 4
The Ladder of the Beatitudes I:
Beginning the Ascent. 26
Jane Bensman

CHAPTER 5
The Ladder of the Beatitudes II:
Embracing the Challenge 33
Norm Rich

CHAPTER 6
Principles of Discernment 40
Fr. James Schimelpfening, SM

CHAPTER 7
Becoming a Beatitude Community 48
Sr. Angela Ann Zukowski, MHSH

ABOUT THE CONTRIBUTORS 56

RECOMMENDED RESOURCES 57

INTRODUCTION

Blessed are the poor in spirit,
    for theirs is the kingdom of heaven.
Blessed are they who mourn,
    for they will be comforted.
Blessed are the meek,
    for they will inherit the land.
Blessed are they who hunger and thirst for righteousness,
    for they will be satisfied.
Blessed are the merciful,
    for they will be shown mercy.
Blessed are the clean of heart,
    for they will see God.
Blessed are the peacemakers,
    for they will be called children of God.
Blessed are they who are persecuted for the sake of righteousness,
    for theirs is the kingdom of heaven.
Blessed are you when they insult you and persecute you and utter every kind of evil against you [falsely] because of me. Rejoice and be glad, for your reward will be great in heaven. MATTHEW 5:3-12

Imagine what it must have been like nearly 2,000 years ago to be part of a large crowd listening to an itinerant preacher describe the qualities and actions of people especially blessed by God— among them, the poor in spirit, the meek, the persecuted. Even today, we scratch our heads and wonder at the paradoxes found in Jesus' Beatitudes. This book helps us deepen our adult understanding of Jesus' Sermon on the Mount, and it enriches our understanding of how Jesus calls his disciples to live.

1

The BEATITUDES: OUR MORAL COMPASS

DAVID WHEELER-REED

Almost every biblical scholar I know says that the Sermon on the Mount is Jesus' template for what it means to live life in the Kingdom of God.

Every time I think of the Sermon on the Mount, I am reminded of two quotes. The first is from a pacifist farmer from Kentucky named Wendell Berry. In his book *Citizenship Papers* (Berkeley, CA: Counterpoint Press, 2003), he says that the best advice we as human beings were ever given is found in the Sermon on the Mount. But he also notes that this template for human progress is the least obeyed.

I also think of the French peasant Peter Maurin, who was the intellectual guru behind the Catholic Worker movement. In his *Easy Essays* (Yonkers, NY: Rose Hill Books, 2003), he writes, "When the Sermon on the Mount is the standard of values, then Christ is the leader." Unfortunately, in our own day and age—even in our own church—it often feels as if the Sermon on the Mount is not our moral compass. Rather, it is more a mere suggestion than divine fiat concerning what our Lord expects of us.

Almost every biblical scholar I know says that the Sermon on the Mount is Jesus' template for what it means to live life in the Kingdom of God. It is not just about how we as Christians interact with the larger world of which we are a part. It also is about how we as Christians treat one another as sisters and brothers in Christ.

What He Says, What He Doesn't Say

Matthew sets out the major themes of the Sermon on the Mount with what we call the Beatitudes, found in Matthew 5:3–12. It is important for us to notice what Jesus says here—and what he does not say. For instance, as a poor peasant from Nazareth, Jesus blesses the "poor in spirit," or what today we would call "those who are spiritually down and out." He blesses those who mourn, those who hunger, and those who promote peace.

But he never once blesses those who are violent, those who are rich, those who persecute, or those who refuse to show mercy. I also have been struck by the fact that never once in the Sermon on the Mount does Jesus approve of any governmental authority, nor does he bless the religious hierarchy of Jerusalem. I can only wonder what we are to make of this today.

When I reflect on these things, I am often reminded of something the Jewish scholar Pinchas Lapide said. In his little book titled *Sermon on the Mount: Utopia or Program for Action?* (Maryknoll, NY: Orbis Books, Rev. 1986), Lapide expresses bewilderment at Christians who think they are better off under grace than under Jewish Law. He tells his readers that after reading the Sermon on the Mount he came to the conclusion that he would rather be bound to the 613 commandments of the Torah because grace looks really hard!

Although many Christians may not be prepared to hear this, Lapide suggests that the Sermon on the Mount is a summons to give up everything and follow Jesus, even if it means losing one's life. He also notes that Jesus' radical teachings in the Sermon on the Mount would set him apart from many of the later rabbis of the Jewish Talmud.

Do We Take Him Seriously?

I often find myself wondering if we take Jesus seriously. Do we take him seriously when he talks about anger (Matthew 5:21–26)? Do we take him seriously when he tells us that being angry at a sister or brother makes us a candidate for judgment? How often do we think before we call a sister or a brother "a fool"?

I am often puzzled by Christians who speak in mean ways about other Christians, especially politicians. Moreover, when I go to restaurants and watch folks clasping their hands together or crossing themselves in public, my mind returns to Matthew 6:6, "But when you pray, go to your inner room, close the door, and pray to your Father in secret. And your Father who sees in secret will repay you." When I go to our megamalls or megachurches or chain restaurants, I am often haunted by Jesus' words that "No one can serve two masters... You cannot serve God and mammon [money]" (Matthew 6:24).

> The Beatitudes, however, are not promises of future redemption. They are promises of present redemption.

In the Sermon on the Mount, Jesus teaches his disciples the Lord's Prayer. But unlike Luke's version of the Lord's Prayer, Matthew's Jesus gives us a little bit of extra commentary. In Matthew 6:14–15, Jesus says, "If you forgive others their transgressions, your heavenly Father will forgive you. But if you do not forgive others, neither will your Father forgive your transgressions."

The early church took this admonition seriously. The early Christians knew that to forgive was conditional; to ask for forgiveness from God meant showing mercy to those who had caused Christians hurt and pain.

It is easy to see why Pinchas Lapide thought Jewish Law was easier than Jesus' teachings on grace.

The Beatitudes, however, are not promises of future redemption. They are promises of present redemption. The Greek translation of the

Beatitudes tells us that "those who mourn" will be "comforted right now!" and that "those who hunger and thirst for justice" will be "satisfied right now!" It is no wonder, then, that spiritual masters like Gandhi and civil rights leaders like Martin Luther King Jr., found in the Sermon on the Mount a moral compass for a new world that was possible even in the present.

Practical Suggestions

I would like to make some practical suggestions as to how we might implement the Sermon on the Mount in our own lives. I will limit myself, of course, to the Beatitudes, but any of my suggestions could easily be used in any part of the Sermon.

We must identify with the "poor in spirit."

This term is a tricky one, which eluded scholars until the discovery of the Dead Sea Scrolls. The poor in spirit is a Hebrew idiom that means "those who have been beaten down by the vicissitudes of life." To put it another way, it is a term that describes those who have experienced the "injustice" of an unfair world.

Since, as Christians, we are already part of the "new creation" (Galatians 6:15), there is no need for us to wait for Christ to bring justice to this world at a future, unknown date. As ambassadors of Jesus, we can start working with Jesus right now by promoting justice in our own churches, by identifying with people who are crushed by life, and by lending a helping hand to anyone in need.

One suggestion I would offer is, for those of us who have the financial resources, to adopt a family who struggles financially or to pay for healthcare for someone who doesn't have it. Or we could be even more radical and tell a pregnant teen contemplating abortion that we will do all that we can to help her financially so that she may keep her baby and bring life, not death, into the world.

We can help comfort those "who mourn" right now.
I often have been amazed at how the simplest acts of kindness can change people. Instead of just tossing some coins at people who ask for money on the street, we can sit down with these persons, listen to their stories, and perhaps invite them to share a meal with us.

If we were to choose a more radical path, we might take the suggestion of Peter Maurin and make up a room in our homes called a "Christ room," where anyone who comes knocking throughout the day or night can find a bed, a shower, and a hot breakfast in the morning.

We can ask ourselves if injustice makes us sick.
Are we the kind of people "who hunger and thirst for justice," or are we the kind of people who turn blind eyes away from injustices? I have been disturbed recently by the number of Christians who say, "God is in control. All I need do is pray." I do not doubt that God is in control, but we must never forget that God also asks us to work together with Jesus to further the Kingdom of God on earth.

We can ask ourselves, "Are we merciful?"
Do we call our opponents "blessed enemies" or do we call them "fools"? Do we gossip and ridicule a fellow sister or brother? Do we heap harangue after harangue on the heads of politicians and pundits who need our prayers more than our criticisms?

We can ask ourselves, "Are we peacemakers?"
Does each and every action we take promote discord or unity? Do we participate in acts of violence, or do we eschew violence entirely? Do we support a political system that leads to war, or do we do everything we can to make sure that future generations never need to know the horrors we have known in our own generation or in generations past?

We need to ask ourselves a very difficult question: "Are we being insulted and persecuted, or are we just plain comfortable?" In the Sermon on the Mount, there is a call from Jesus to let go of our comfort and to engage the world in ways that ultimately lead to persecution and criticism—from both the church and the world. The Kingdom of Heaven does not belong to those who are "just plain comfortable," but to those who seek justice and, as a consequence, experience the world's wrath.

> Does each and every action we take promote discord or unity?

So we must ask ourselves, "Why are we not being persecuted? Why are we not being criticized? Have we become too comfortable? Are we trying to change things or are we simply part of the system?"

Conclusion

I know a devout Catholic who gets very upset with me when I talk about Jesus' moral compass in the Sermon on Mount. He often interjects, "This is impossible. No one could do this. Surely Jesus was not being serious!"

This man is very pragmatic, so I often tell him, "We must realize that Jesus is not very pragmatic! In fact, some might say he was irrational—perhaps even criminal!" I then remind him of what Pinchas Lapide said: "The law is easy, but grace is hard!"

Your Thoughts

1 How do I understand the Sermon on the Mount to be the moral compass in my life? How often do I refer to this moral compass in my ordinary day-to-day choices? (Be specific.)

_____

_____

_____

2 What is my perspective on "The law is easy, but grace is hard"?

_____

_____

_____

Try This

Identify a practice for living the Sermon on the Mount in a meaningful manner. Write a personal contract for incorporating a new Beatitude way of living.

The FOUNDATION for LIVING the BEATITUDES

SEAN REYNOLDS

It's not that the Beatitudes are meant to replace the Ten Commandments. Rather, the Beatitudes perfect the Commandments....

Did you know that in order for a GPS to tell you where you are, it needs at least three satellites to get a basic "fix" on your location? Christian morality isn't too different. We Christians typically rely on at least three "sites" in the Scriptures to get a fix on how to live: the Ten Commandments, Jesus' Great Commandments, and the Beatitudes, in which we are welcomed into the very heart of Jesus' teaching.

The *Catechism of the Catholic Church* (CCC) puts the Beatitudes in a place of priority near the beginning of the section on moral living (Part 3, "Life in Christ," nos. 1716-1729) with this explanation: "The Beatitudes are at the heart of Jesus' preaching. They take up the promises made to the chosen people since Abraham. The Beatitudes fulfill the promises by ordering them no longer merely to the possession of a territory, but to the Kingdom of heaven..." (n. 1716).

It's not that the Beatitudes are meant to replace the Ten Commandments. Rather, the Beatitudes perfect the Commandments, as Jesus said: "Do not think that I have come to abolish the law or the prophets. I have come not to abolish but to fulfill" (Matthew 5:17). Without the Beatitudes, catechesis on the Commandments will likely miss the mark.

Situating the Beatitudes in Sacred Scriptures

Carefully and prayerfully read the Beatitudes from Matthew 5:3–12 (see page 1). Blessed are those who are poor in spirit, who mourn, who hunger and thirst. Surely Jesus can't be serious! Further, the Greek word for blessed, *makarios*, can also be translated "happy," which induces more incredulity: How can it be that happiness results from mourning, meekness, and poverty?

> It is clear that the Ten Commandments are only a starting point for moral formation. Jesus calls his followers to so much more....

Obviously, there is a deeper wisdom here, to be understood in its broader context in Matthew's gospel. Scripture scholars agree that "the kingdom of heaven" is the centerpiece of Jesus' teaching in Matthew. The Beatitudes are a central part of Jesus' larger teaching on the kingdom of heaven, which is mysteriously both now and not yet, both heavenly and "at hand" (Matthew 3:2; 4:17).

So in the Beatitudes (the heart of the Sermon on the Mount), our GPS locates us in the living heart of God. We have in Matthew's Beatitudes a description of discipleship, a snapshot of the desired outcome(s) of all our catechesis: people who live with God/Christ/Spirit at the center of their lives, and whose lives provide salt, light, and leaven for the life of the world. The integrity and authenticity in their discipleship lead them to be peacemakers, to suffer rejection for righteousness' sake, to bring to the world purity of heart, mercy, and above all, love.

Thus it is clear that the Ten Commandments are only a starting point for moral formation. Jesus calls his followers to so much more: a life of

11

abundant blessing and happiness, as described in John's gospel: "I came so that they might have life and have it more abundantly" (10:10).

The Blessing, Now and for All Time

This isn't the so-called "prosperity gospel" of today's TV preachers. Luke's Beatitudes clearly say otherwise (Luke 6:20–26). To his "blessed," Luke adds a series of "woes" that serve to sharpen the message: "But woe to you who are rich, for you have received your consolation. But woe to you who are filled now, for you will be hungry. Woe to you who laugh now, for you will grieve and weep. Woe to you when all speak well of you, for their ancestors treated the false prophets in this way" (Luke 6:24–26).

In short, those who look to the things of this world to fill the void that only God can fill will experience woe instead of blessing and happiness. Living in Christ is its own blessing. In fact, *the* blessing, now and for all time. And those who are lost (i.e., with one's inner GPS obstructed or simply switched off) live the woe of separation from God.

Both Matthew and Luke declare the universal message of Jesus: The kingdom of heaven is here, now, available, and free. All we need do is live in it and live it out. The Beatitudes show us what this living looks like.

Obstacles to Living the Beatitudes

We live in a country that calls itself Christian but serves up a very different popular gospel. The very temptations that Jesus rejected in the desert—namely wealth, prestige, and power—have become the secular altars at which many Americans worship.

Moreover, the role of faith and religion in young people in the United States is diminishing. Whether Catholic, Protestant, or Jewish, youth are adopting a watered-down belief system: God exists to make us happy, and God wants us to be nice; and nice people go to heaven.

The research says that this belief system is like a cancer gradually replacing the healthy cells of faith with a trivial and impotent substitute, not just in young people but in their parents and families as well.

So What Must We Do?

It seems we have our work cut out for us. Here are some suggestions:

> Whether Catholic, Protestant, or Jewish, youth are adopting a watered-down belief system....

Live the Beatitudes.

We have in our humble possession the most precious of all gifts: abundant life in God. Yet, we need to ask ourselves: Are we living the Beatitudes or are we snared in conventional assumptions about what's important, about success, power, and prestige? If we are of a divided mind, we'll necessarily share ambivalence instead of the boldness of "those who are persecuted for the sake of righteousness."

Put simply, God wants our happiness, and God is our happiness. Are we living the life God wants for us or do we need to return and drink long and deeply at the well of grace that is the bottomless font of our catechesis—via prayer, the sacraments, scriptural and spiritual reading, with spiritual companions, on retreat, day in and day out?

Teach the Beatitudes.

The good news of the Beatitudes falls often on deaf ears, perhaps because it's so countercultural. How then do we convey the message so it's heard, understood, and integrated into life? Here are some ideas:

- *Study the saints.* Learning about the saints can lead to lives guided by the Beatitudes. Pope Francis took his name from St. Francis of Assisi, whose story perhaps more than any other shines with the joy, freedom, and true happiness that come from a life lived in Christ. As a young man, St. Francis gave himself to Christ and, in doing so, rejected a life of wealth and influence. The stories of his life are colorful and capture the imagination, perhaps like no other saint. Consider inviting Franciscans to come to your class to tell stories of St. Francis and explain his significance in our lives today.

- *Nurture stillness.* The Chinese character for "busy" is a combination of two characters: heart and killing. In our entertainment-saturated society, incessant activity has become the norm and busyness a bizarre badge of pride. The result? People crave quiet, yet resist it.

  Happily, there is some good news in this: Our restlessness can lead to first-person encounters with Christ if we simply get quiet enough to pay attention. In his *Confessions*, St. Augustine said, "You have made us for yourself, O Lord, and our hearts are restless until they rest in you." How are we cultivating stillness and listening in our lives and in ministry? (Consider the story of Elijah in 1 Kings 19:11–13, in which he finally hears God in "a light silent sound.")

  Creating time and space for quiet attention can be fruitful in our ministry. Perhaps instead of a prayer at the beginning or end of a gathering, we need extended prayer and meditation times in our sessions—without packing those times with readings, music, and talk. Sometimes extended programs like retreats are the only way to break the addictive patterns of busyness and distractions.

  > In our entertainment-saturated society, incessant activity has become the norm and busyness a bizarre badge of pride.

- *Reclaim Sabbath.* For many of us Catholics, "keeping holy the Sabbath" has been reduced to going to Mass—that's all. Wayne Muller's book *Sabbath: Restoring the Sacred Rhythm of Rest* (New York: Bantam Books, 2000) provides reflection exercises and the wisdom to counter the toxicity of our overly busy lives.

- *Witness.* Consider tapping personal stories that contrast with the conventional assumptions about success and point, instead, toward a life lived in Christ. In other words, invite as speakers individuals who have left high-paying jobs in order to serve the poor, who have walked away from money or prestige so as to pursue principle and compassion—people whose lives preach the Beatitudes.

How do you find these people? If simply asking around doesn't work, contact your diocesan mission office and inquire about religious and lay missionaries. It's best if they're ordinary people whose decisions and lives can't be explained away because they're somehow different or special.

- *Study modern-day saintly persons.* Although they are not canonized, modern-day saintly persons powerfully portray the Beatitudes. Three with movies and/or documentaries made of their lives are Dorothy Day, Archbishop Oscar Romero, and Sr. Dorothy Stang, SND.

- *Immersion experiences.* Immersion experiences in service, peace, and justice can be moments of conversion when an individual can get perspective, examine assumptions, and make fresh and freer decisions for Christ. One need not leave the country for such experiences. They're available in our inner cities and immigrant neighborhoods and among the rural poor.

- *Examinations of conscience.* Help people prepare for the sacrament of reconciliation through the Beatitudes, emphasizing not just how we've sinned but how we're following Christ and might better do so.

Conclusion

A final caution—and prayer: We don't "do" the Beatitudes as if they were a set of moral prescriptions. They are what God does *in us* as we grow in Christ and become his heart and hands: "The Spirit of the Lord is upon me, because he has anointed me to bring glad tidings to the poor. He has sent me to proclaim liberty to captives and recovery of sight to the blind, to let the oppressed go free, and to proclaim a year acceptable to the Lord" (Luke 4:18–19).

Cultivating the Beatitudes in others will happen by God's grace. This is a great consolation: We are but humble messengers. Let us pray that by God's grace we find ourselves blessed among the poor and meek, and happy among those who hunger and thirst for righteousness, for theirs is the Kingdom of Heaven.

Your Thoughts

1 Does the metaphor of a GPS as a guide for
Christian morality connect with me? How and why?

_____

_____

_____

_____

2 "Without the Beatitudes, catechesis on the
Commandments will likely miss the mark." What does
this mean for how I catechize?

_____

_____

_____

Try This

Write an examination of conscience based on the
Beatitudes (Sermon on the Mount). Integrate this examination of conscience into your daily life.

PORTRAIT *and* PROMISE *of* DISCIPLESHIP

SUSAN K. SACK

What does God want of you? A simple question—but perhaps not easy to answer. Probably the best response to what God asks of us is "to love as Jesus loved, to deny ourselves, and to follow him." God wants us to become disciples.

The sacrament of baptism initiates us into the life of discipleship. *Discipleship* comes from the word *discipline*, which implies a certain way of life. As baptized Christian disciples, we are to practice Jesus' way of life—particularly that which Jesus describes in the Beatitudes.

Each of us is called to this. This vocation isn't just for monks or nuns or deacons or even lay ministers or catechists. It is for all of us who desire to have God in our lives, who long to become the people we are meant to be. It is about shedding our religious mediocrity for holiness, a holiness that grows daily as we increasingly "put on" Jesus.

We are to be people who hear and obey the voice of God by putting the word into action in our lives, witnessing and proclaiming God's love to the world.

Called to Perfect Holiness

One of the great documents of the Second Vatican Council, the *Dogmatic Constitution on the Church* (*Lumen Gentium*) tells us that, whatever our state in life, we are all called by God to perfect holiness. We are called to the holiness expressed in the Beatitudes, for they describe what disciples are to do now, as well as who they will become if they follow Jesus.

The Beatitudes are a portrait of what discipleship is about. The Beatitudes act as a compass for those on the journey of Christian discipleship. Live this way, and you are indeed blessed.

It certainly is easy to lose direction today, so we need a compass! In the past, things seemed much more clear-cut. The Christian way of life wasn't questioned nearly so much. Families participated in the sacraments on a regular basis, followed the commandments, and listened to the church leaders. Distinct expectations existed. Now, generally, nothing seems expected; life becomes what we make up as we go along.

> Is it possible to be meek or to be a peacemaker and still survive? Is it even possible to be disciples?

So it can be very difficult to know how to be "poor in Spirit" in this free-form world of competitive, consumerist glee. Is it possible to be meek or to be a peacemaker and still survive? Is it even possible to be disciples?

For those determined to respond to God's call in the affirmative and to live a Beatitude discipleship, this chapter suggests that four characteristics seem crucial. These attributes are interwoven and build on each other. Disciples (1) are rooted in Scripture and prayer; (2) live a life of integrity; (3) express compassion through action; and (4) undergo life-long conversion.

1. Disciples Are Rooted in Scripture and Prayer

The contemporary world is a constant stream of words and images, so it can be difficult to sort out what is important and what can be overlooked. As Christian disciples, we have a primary task to be willing to listen, to open our hearts so that we can bring God's word into our own world. God can then shape our world.

How can we know how to live the Beatitudes if we don't know what the Beatitudes say? This involves more than just reading Scripture. Discipleship really occurs when the word read becomes the word lived in our daily lives. That transformation occurs through prayer.

> Discipleship really occurs when the word read becomes the word lived in our daily lives.

Prayer is the expression of our relationship with God. This relationship grows through prayer and through Scripture. Beyond that, prayer is difficult to define, as it can take so many different forms. In fact, prayer takes on almost as many forms as the number of pray-ers—as each of us prays in our own manner and in different ways at different times in our lives.

Surveys tell us that almost everyone prays in at least some rudimentary fashion. For disciples, prayer, like reading Scripture, can be neither rudimentary nor optional. Disciples who wish to live Beatitude lives must make prayer central to life.

So as disciples, we must commit ourselves to reading Scripture and praying regularly, both privately and communally. Yet, few Catholics actually do this. Why? Probably the primary reason is fear.

The Bible is a huge and complex book! How does one even know where to start? Also, both prayer and Scripture make demands of those of us who pay attention. They cause us to reconsider our worldview. It can be tough to do this, so why put ourselves through it?

Yet, with prayer and Scripture, we are swept into the consciousness of those things that are of God. We begin to recognize, or to discern, certain moments in life as "of God." God is then not only at the center of life but, in a sense, God becomes life and all life becomes prayer. Our knowl-

edge of what discipleship is about and how
to better practice it also expands.

On a regular basis, too, disciples should
ask if their prayer brings further conversion
toward Christ. As the stories of the saints tell
us, at certain points in our lives we will be
asked to move deeper into prayer, toward
further transformation of our lives in and
toward God.

> Discipleship is
> about trusting that
> God alone can fill
> up the emptiness
> we experience
> and give us the
> security we desire.

Pick up Scripture and Read It!

If you don't have a good study Bible, find one that has some background information so that you are better able to understand the social
and historical context of each book. (The United States bishops recommend the *New American Bible, Revised Edition*, 2011.) Consider finding
a group of fellow parishioners or catechists with whom to study, and
commit to finding a trained, competent person to whom you can go
with questions.

Perhaps you might want to investigate some of the traditional forms
of prayer that start with Scripture, such as *lectio divina*, the Liturgy of the
Hours, or the Eucharist. The Eucharist is the pinnacle of Christian life
and the type of communal prayer in which each disciple should participate regularly.

2. Disciples Live Lives of Integrity

It's one thing to say discipleship is about holiness, prayer, and Scripture,
but it's another thing to know what holiness looks like. In comparison
to much of society, most of us probably think we are "good enough." So
we can't all be the monk praying in a cell or a martyr giving our life for
Christ. But isn't intermittent reading of the Bible and Mass on Sunday
enough?

When the word of God becomes the basis of life, then disciples
should increasingly reflect the being of God. The Beatitudes make just

that argument: God must be seen in our actions and our attitudes. Having lived in God's word and expressed that relationship with God through prayer, disciples reflect and faithfully live out that word.

Discipleship means we will incorporate into our behavior the primary qualities of God, including generosity, mercy, and forgiveness. This fidelity to God means we must be willing to examine regularly both our internal and external lives, with Jesus as the model for our actions. We must develop the habit of reflecting on our daily lives.

One aspect of this examination is to ask what it is we are "living for." Do we live for God's kingdom rather than for ourselves? Do we fill up the emptiness and self-doubt we sometimes feel with material things, with a scrambling for more privileged positions, with addictive behavior? Is it even possible for us to be meek and poor and recognize the longing we feel for God? Discipleship is about trusting that God alone can fill up the emptiness we experience and give us the security we desire.

So living a life of integrity implies that it should be easy for us to find evidence of the importance of God. Or do we, instead, live as if nothing of the gospel matters? Are we sure that "religion" means being nice, not causing scandal, and doing what is expected? Is God simply the God of comfort rather than sometimes the God of challenges? Which is the God of the Beatitudes?

3. Disciples Express Compassion through Action

In a world so incredibly individualized, the greatest human need today may simply be having someone walk with us. Disciples aren't just individuals; discipleship is about a community. We become the Mystical Body of Christ in the church, the body of Jesus extended through space and time. In that body, we are part of Christ and yet also part of one another. We share one another's burdens and joys. This union of the body stands in countercultural testimony to the individualism and impersonal nature of contemporary society.

Many of today's sins arise from the rejection of this connectedness. Our culture teaches us to use others for our own purposes, to distance ourselves emotionally and physically, to pursue our own good rather than the common good.

Yet, when we share our burdens through the Corporal and Spiritual Works of Mercy, as expressed in the Beatitudes, we see evidence that we are meant to live beyond ourselves. We transcend our limited existence to somehow become one with all the earth. We see that we can act out of love, even when it brings nothing to us personally.

> The discipline of carrying another's cross makes the carrying much easier for everyone.

The discipline of carrying another's cross makes the carrying much easier for everyone. When we feel "with" others, we grow spiritually so that the burdens of our own lives do not weigh as heavily. We become more vulnerable, open, and as St. Irenaeus said, "more fully alive" and more fully like God.

Let's face it: Sitting back and criticizing the world leads only to more frustration. The world can only be changed by people willing to work to change it. Reaching out to that imperfect world is a real test of the sincerity of our discipleship.

More so than writing a check (although that certainly has its place), exposing our bodies, hearts, and spirits to the suffering that can exist in the world, without any expectation of reward, is the disciple's way to walk the path of Jesus. It also continuously forms us in the love of a God who sent his Son to do the same thing.

4. Disciples Undergo Continuing Conversion

The last step required in Beatitude discipleship is a commitment to ongoing conversion. We are born learners, and we continue to learn throughout life—sometimes despite our best efforts to do otherwise. We blunder on, attempting to better understand who we are and who we are meant to be. Human life is a journey toward greater truths, toward further discovery of our inner selves and our outer worlds.

The road can be narrow or bumpy or full of detours. When it comes to relationships, including our relationship with God, we definitely learn through trial and error. It is hard to know what is truly good for ourselves and those we love. What comes from self-centeredness and what comes from sincere and loving motives?

This is the journey Jesus asks us to walk as disciples who recognize the truth of the way of the Beatitudes. We are to learn to love others for their own sake with the love that God has—a generous, reciprocal, non-manipulative, and universal love.

> When it comes to relationships, including our relationship with God, we definitely learn through trial and error.

Like the Apostles, we don't get it right the first time, or maybe even the hundredth time. It's as much about learning forgiveness and reconciliation (including learning to forgive ourselves) as about joy and togetherness.

We hurt terribly sometimes. As the Beatitudes and the Paschal Mystery imply, we will experience suffering, maybe persecution, and eventually death. Still, God always and lovingly strengthens us with perseverance and leads us to the deeper levels of discipleship. There, if we are willing, we come more fully into communion with God, where hope and life are eternal.

Conclusion

This is what God asks of us: to become disciples of the God who wishes union with us. This way is rooted in Scripture and prayer, forms our life into one of integrity, calls us to compassionate action in the world, and is a lifelong turning toward God. As the Beatitudes express, if we agree to follow Jesus, our difficulties, weaknesses, and efforts eventually are transcended by the Kingdom of God. Discipleship truly is a way of blessedness.

Your Thoughts

1 Do I consider myself a disciple of Christ? Why?

_____

_____

_____

2 Which of the four characteristics of a Beatitude disciple is the most difficult for me to put into practice? Why?

_____

_____

_____

Try This

Discuss with other catechists how elements of the RCIA might be adapted into your catechetical program at various levels. How might this experience enrich both teachers' and students' understanding and appreciation of discipleship?

The LADDER of the BEATITUDES I: BEGINNING the ASCENT

JANE BENSMAN

A first step on the ladder of the Beatitudes can be the beginning of an ascent to a whole new way of life or a deeper commitment to continue to grow in relationship with the Lord.

We have all heard the statement: "The first step is the hardest!" That first step can be the hardest whether we are trying to change a habit or begin a new way of life. Seeing the Beatitudes arranged on a ladder, as presented by Jim Forest in his book titled *The Ladder of the Beatitudes* (Maryknoll, NY: Orbis Books, 1999) is a good visual image of how difficult it can be to take that first step to live the Beatitudes intentionally.

Climbing a ladder can be scary, especially if we are afraid of heights. Reaching the top, however, can give us quite a sense of accomplishment. A first step on the ladder of the Beatitudes can be the beginning of an ascent to a whole new way of life or a deeper commitment to continue to grow in relationship with the Lord.

This chapter explores the meaning of the first four Beatitudes on the rungs of the Beatitude ladder—meanings that have a real relationship to day-to-day living as a Catholic Christian.

Understanding "Poor in Spirit"

"Blessed are the poor in spirit for theirs is the kingdom of heaven" (Matthew 5:3). The first step in embracing this Beatitude is the most important if we are to continue on the Beatitude ladder. We can be poor physically, emotionally, or spiritually—none of which is easy to experience.

For some, being poor happens as a result of circumstances in society. For others, being poor is a decision (for example, Dorothy Day). But to be truly poor in spirit, I believe, happens gradually.

After doing everything we can to be comfortable, happy, and in control, we gradually realize that the only thing we can depend on for sure is God's love and care for us. Even those who are very wealthy can be poor in spirit because being poor in spirit means approaching God with a destitution of spirit, a longing to know God's will.

> Being poor in spirit means entering into a relationship with Jesus that is freeing and loving.

Learning how to be poor in spirit means living and walking in the light of Christ, like the man born blind in the Scriptures. The man was healed and saw that he was in the presence of the Son of God, the Light of the World—and the man's world changed. In contrast, a person who is materially poor is not necessarily poor in spirit if he or she continually longs for more and is jealous of those who have more. A person is truly poor in spirit only when he or she recognizes that only God can fulfill all needs.

St. Teresa of Calcutta said that the greatest poverty is lack of faith and being closed in on oneself. Being poor in spirit means entering into a relationship with Jesus that is freeing and loving. Each of us has been created to be loved. We experience that love in human relationships because it already exists in the love God has for us and our human ability to share this love with others.

Choosing to love in this way includes making a choice to live in relationships over independence. Although there is a push for independence while we're growing up, we eventually recognize that we are dependent on God and others.

Choosing to live in relationships over independence requires loving others as God loves—rather than manipulating others for our own happiness. At times, it even means submission—with love and respect for one another. Christ gave up his independence and died on the cross for us because he loved us.

So you might wonder: If I can continually work toward being poor in spirit, what is that "Kingdom of God" I will experience? It is an experience of freedom now and ultimately in eternity. We experience a freedom on this earth—a freedom to stop judging and being judged and trying to change others to fit our standards. We experience mercy, forgiveness, and the freedom to live fully and love all God's creation with no agenda.

We see Christ's presence and experience his grace, even in the midst of suffering. We walk in the light of Christ. A Franciscan motto says: "The joy of poverty is not to have nothing in this world; the joy of poverty is to have nothing but God."

Understanding "Mourning"

"Blessed are they who mourn, for they will be comforted" (Matthew 5:4). Being poor in spirit is inseparable from mourning. We mourn for ourselves—the sins in our lives and the missed opportunities to turn to Christ—and we mourn for and with others.

We mourn those times when we depended on other resources instead of on God. Without a poverty of spirit, we can never completely let our guard down and give freely of everything we have.

Poverty of spirit opens us to the pain of others. Our tears with and for others are Christ's tears. When we mourn, we must become transparent and open, sharing our pain and loss so we can become compassionate in our understanding of the mourning of those around us.

While death and illness are common experiences of mourning, this Beatitude opens us to mourning for those who are hungry, homeless, persecuted, depressed, and mentally ill. We mourn for those who have turned their backs on God and on so many other things; we do not judge them, we mourn for them.

> When we mourn we have an ally, a helper, in the Holy Spirit, who exhorts and encourages us to do that which we thought impossible.

Jesus used the Greek word *parakalein* for the word "comfort" in this Beatitude. This word means not only to comfort but also to encourage, excite, and urge. Those who mourn will be witnesses to others. As in Acts 2:1–4, after the Holy Spirit—the Paraclete, the Comforter—descended on the Apostles, they burst forth from hiding, ready to be witnesses.

In the same way, those who mourn will be on fire to be comforters to others and to witness to God's faithfulness. When we mourn we have an ally, a helper, in the Holy Spirit, who exhorts and encourages us to do that which we thought impossible.

Those of us who mourn are comforted in knowing that Christ is always inviting us to a banquet—not just a banquet where we will be comforted but a banquet where we will be fed and nourished. When we have mourned and found comfort from God, we can be with others who mourn, not to take away their mourning and grief but to help them endure it and, being poor in spirit, turn to God for comfort.

Understanding "Meek"

"Blessed are the meek, for they will inherit the land" (Matthew 5:5). *Meek* is not a word that most people think sounds like something they want to be. Yet the definition of *meek* is: "one who disciplines self to be gentle, rather than severe; non-violent; bears reproaches and slights; is not bent on revenge; is free from bitterness and belligerence; is tranquil and steady of spirit."

The definition of the word *meek* says nothing about being weak or being a doormat for others. It also does not say that we can never be angry about injustice. Rather, being meek means knowing when to get angry and what to do with that anger.

Jesus got angry at those who were self-righteous and hypocritical. He didn't get angry at those who plotted to arrest him, betrayed him, or denied him. Rather, Jesus was meek. There are many examples in Scripture of Jesus' meekness. "I am meek and humble of heart" (Matthew 11:29); "Yet not as I will, but as you will" (Matthew 26:39); "Forgive them, they know not what they do" (Luke 23:34).

Being meek means believing that goodness can come out of any calamity. It means knowing what to do with our anger in ways that we will inherit the earth.

Understanding "Hunger and Thirst"

"Blessed are they who hunger and thirst for righteousness, for they will be satisfied" (Matthew 5:6). This Beatitude does not say we "hope" for righteousness; rather, it says we "hunger and thirst"—we hunger and thirst for righteousness as much as we hunger and thirst for food and drink.

Hungering and thirsting for righteousness is a profound longing for life to be on earth as it is in heaven—which we know is impossible, and yet we long for and work for that kind of life. A righteous person is someone in whom others, especially those in need, experience the mercy and love of God.

How can this hunger and thirst be satisfied? First, we discern our gifts and talents and develop them for service and in praise for God. Then we use our gifts and talents to support those laws, agencies, and organizations that help and protect the needy in our society. We stand with those who often stand alone in our families, neighborhoods, churches, and world.

In living this Beatitude, we do not just wish for something to happen; rather, we become consumed with the desire to be part of making something happen according to God's plan and will for all people.

What is the satisfaction we can experience as a person who longs for righteousness? Some days we will be very satisfied with the fulfillment of God's promise through our own works and the work of others according to God's plan. Other days we will continue to hunger and thirst.

> We stand with those who often stand alone in our families, neighborhoods, churches, and world.

At the end of the day, we will be satisfied that our primary focus was not on food or possessions but on a life in unity with God, a life transformed by love and poor in spirit. While we will never be fully satisfied on this earth, we at least can be grateful that we were awakened to the hunger and the thirst.

Conclusion

How do we increase in our practice of living the Beatitudes? One thought is to view the virtues needed for the Beatitudes as muscles: the more we exercise them the more they will increase in strength. Additionally, calling upon the Holy Spirit to fill us with the Spirit's gifts and fruits will strengthen us.

Neuroscientists have discovered that feeling compassion causes part of the nervous system to light up, including parts of the frontal brain lobes—our emotional control center. It is also associated with the release of oxytocin, the "tend and befriend" hormone that helps calm stress and boosts immune function.

So on a scientific level, we could say that living the Beatitudes boosts our physical health. On a spiritual level, living the Beatitudes gives us the best possible chance to one day hear the words: "Well done, my good and faithful servant" (Matthew 25:21, 23).

Your Thoughts

1 What does the metaphor of a ladder for understanding the Beatitudes say to me? How does it enrich my appreciation and understanding of the Beatitudes?

_____

_____

_____

2 What does "Blessed are the poor in spirit for theirs is the kingdom of heaven" mean for me? How can I exercise this Beatitude?

_____

_____

_____

Try This

Prayerfully read and reflect on the first four Beatitudes (Matthew 5:3–6). Then journal about what personal message, challenge, or invitation you receive for living these Beatitudes.

5

The LADDER *of the* BEATITUDES II: EMBRACING *the* CHALLENGE

NORM RICH

In this chapter, we examine the Beatitudes that remind us of the possibility of persecution, yet call us to be merciful, pure of heart, and makers of peace so we may climb closer to the top of the ladder where we will experience more fully the presence of God.

The desire of every human being is to be happy. We might say we want wealth or fame or power, but we only mention these things because we believe these things will make us happy. In the gospels, however, it is clear that the path to happiness does not lie in our worldly desires. Rather, it lies in the path set forth in the Beatitudes.

The word *blessed* comes from the Greek word *makarios*, which means "happy." In our culture, happiness is a state of feeling good. In the time of Jesus, however, the word *makarios* reflected the idea of living in harmony with our nature or being in touch with our soul. Since God is love and God created us, we are living according to our nature when we live a life of love. Ultimately, the Beatitudes teach us how to love.

Matthew's gospel states that "whoever loses his life for my sake will save it" (16:25). One common thread found in the three Beatitudes discussed in this article is the challenge to live not for self but for others. Embracing the challenge of the Beatitudes means living beyond ourselves so that we may be merciful, pure of heart, and seekers of peace. Only in embracing this challenge can we live according to our nature and find the happiness that comes from love.

Blessed are the merciful, for they will be shown mercy.

In 1985, Ronald Cotton was identified by Jennifer Thompson as the man who assaulted and raped her. Even though he swore his innocence, he was sentenced to prison where he spent ten years of his life. After DNA evidence exonerated Ronald Cotton of the crime in 1996, Jennifer Thompson asked to meet with him in order to apologize for her grave mistake.

Filled with intense guilt and shame, Jennifer broke down in tears before she could even utter an apology. As tears flowed from Jennifer's eyes, Ronald held her in his arms and said the words she desperately needed to hear: "I forgive you."

When asked by a reporter how he could forgive so easily, Ronald stated that he knew what it was like to lose part of his life and he didn't want Jennifer to lose part of her life feeling guilty for a mistake. The two of them went on to write a book, give talks across the country, and share a common friendship that remains today.

The Greek word for mercy, *eleos*, implies "pouring out" love onto another. One could understand how Ronald Cotton might hold a grudge against a woman who cost him ten years of his life. Yet, he was able to empty himself of anger, resentment, and judgment in order to put himself into the shoes of another fallible human being.

In the Letter of James, we read that "mercy triumphs over judgment" (2:13). In emptying himself, Ronald Cotton was able to extend forgiveness and "pour out" his love on Jennifer.

"Blessed are the merciful" calls us to "forgive those who trespass against us" (see Matthew 6:12) and to love those who hate us. As ministers in the church, we will encounter those who "trespass against us." Like Ronald Cotton, we must be willing to empty ourselves of resentment and put ourselves in the shoes of those to whom we minister. Being ministers to those we like is easy—but this Beatitude calls us to minister to those who resist us as well.

> Augustine reminds us that it is not good enough just to do what is right; we also must think and desire what is right.

Blessed are the clean of heart, for they will see God.

At the turn of the fourth century, a young man named Augustine abandoned the Christian faith of his mother and lived a hedonistic lifestyle. Engaging in sexually promiscuous behavior, drunkenness, and gambling, he took for himself a concubine and had a son out of wedlock. But all of this would change and he would go on to be one of the greatest theologians the Catholic Church has ever known. As revealed in his *Confessions*, it was a change of heart that ultimately led Augustine to give up his unholy lifestyle, embrace celibacy, and commit his life to the church as a bishop.

Augustine embraced the importance of having a "clean heart" as he began to pay attention to his restless soul and the reality that he was not living in accord with his nature. He understood that his lust and selfish desires were leading him to behave in ways that made his life unfulfilling. In his *Confessions* he states: "You have made us for yourself, O Lord, and our hearts are restless until they rest in you" (I, 1).

It was a conversion back to the Christian faith that led Augustine to empty his heart of impurity and allow it to be filled with God's grace.

He knew that to live a life pleasing to God we must begin with what is in our hearts. Thus, his prayer became, "O Holy Spirit, descend plentifully into my heart. Enlighten the dark corners of this neglected dwelling and scatter there Thy cheerful beams."

The Beatitude "Blessed are the clean of heart" reminds us to purge ourselves of unclean thoughts. Augustine reminds us that it is not good enough just to *do* what is right; we also must *think* and *desire* what is right. Matthew's gospel warns that "everyone who looks at a woman with lust has already committed adultery" (5:28). While we may struggle with the idea of being able to sin without action, human nature is such that our actions often flow from our hearts. Many theologians view this passage as Matthew's way of reminding us that cleanliness of heart matters because our hearts will influence what we do.

Being clean of heart requires us to change ourselves, not just our actions. Gandhi once said, "Be the change you seek in the world." Being clean of heart calls us to change, to get rid of our own selfish desires and the pride that prevents us from being honest with ourselves. It requires us to pay attention to the unclean thoughts and feelings we have about others and to challenge them at every turn. When we empty ourselves of our own preoccupations, we can allow God's love to fill us. Only then will we desire what God created us to seek: love.

In dealing with a variety of people as ministers, we naturally make internal judgments. It is easy to act against such judgments in our behavior, but sometimes these judgments can be obstacles to seeing the dignity in those we serve. As ministers in the church, we must challenge ourselves not just to act with love but to think and feel love as well.

**Blessed are the peacemakers,
for they will be called children of God.
Blessed are they who are persecuted,
for theirs is the kingdom of heaven.**
Those were the last words of Sr. Dorothy Stang as she was being murdered. For most of her life, she defended poor farmers in Brazil from

the wealthy ranchers who forged documents and used intimidation to steal land. In 2005, Sister Dorothy was walking to a village that needed her assistance when two hired assassins blocked her route in an effort to intimidate her. Her friend Ciero

> "Love is the only force capable of transforming an enemy into a friend."
>
> **MARTIN LUTHER KING JR.**

was hiding in the bushes when the men tried to scare her into giving up her quest for justice. When asked if she had a weapon, she pulled out her Bible and said, "This is my weapon." As she began to recite the Beatitudes, she was shot and killed.

Being a peacemaker does not mean avoiding conflict. Rather, it means confronting injustice without resorting to violence. Like Sr. Dorothy Stang, it requires us to seek justice and strive for reconciliation in an effort to promote harmony and the common good. Sister Dorothy was a model peacemaker who sought justice for the oppressed without losing sight of God's love for all—even those she fought against. From Sister Dorothy's example, it is clear that being a peacemaker requires courage and perseverance—two qualities that defined this extraordinary woman.

Being a maker of peace also requires us to have mercy and purity of heart—to love our enemies. Martin Luther King Jr., once said, "Love is the only force capable of transforming an enemy into a friend." Sometimes a peacemaker is one who can "transform an enemy into a friend." But there are times when we simply must love our enemy.

Sister Dorothy was also an example of one who was persecuted for the sake of righteousness. A friend of hers told me that she had a stack of threatening letters as high as her desk, yet she had the courage to continue her work. In this Beatitude, Christ reminds all of us that we will be rewarded for our righteousness. If the promise of heaven can give Sister Dorothy the courage to persevere, perhaps we as ministers can endure the more subtle persecution that comes with our vocation.

As ministers in the church, we typically don't face the kind of challenges Sister Dorothy faced, but we do experience conflicts with our colleagues and those we serve. Whether the conflicts involve differences in personality, a clash of ideas, or an instance of miscommunication, this Beatitude requires us to detach ourselves from our own animosity and self-centered goals in order to look at the person with a loving heart.

Conclusion

As we climb the staircase of the Beatitudes, we will experience more fully the presence of God in our lives. Embracing the challenge of the Beatitudes means living beyond ourselves so that we may be merciful, pure of heart, and seekers of peace. It is only in embracing this challenge that we can live according to our nature and find the happiness that comes from love.

Your Thoughts

1 How am I coming to realize that my ascent along the ladder of the Beatitudes is nurturing or can nurture a deeper experience of the presence of God?

_____

_____

_____

2 What personal experience have I had with either forgiving someone or having been forgiven? What impact has this had in my life?

_____

_____

_____

Try This

Identify biblical accounts that articulate reconciliation as the story of God's healing presence in human history. Parallel these biblical accounts to accounts recorded in history today.

6

PRINCIPLES *of* DISCERNMENT

FR. JAMES SCHIMELPFENING, SM

A sacred text is like the flame of a candle. You can observe its color and height....You can measure the intensity of its heat and light, and calculate how rapidly the candle will burn. But...it is not until you have touched your finger to the flame that you can know the real meaning of the candle. This is how it is with sacred texts. **BARBARA E. BOWE, *BIBLICAL FOUNDATIONS OF SPIRITUALITY: TOUCHING A FINGER TO THE FLAME* (WASHINGTON, DC: ROWMAN AND LITTLEFIELD, 2003)**

Becoming a *beatitudinal* person and learning to live a *beatitudinal* life means that we must reach out and "touch the flame" of the Sermon on the Mount—for intellectual understanding alone will not suffice. Touching the flame, however, means being burnt by the word of God and undergoing a change, a shift of consciousness that re-patterns both our inner and outer worlds.

When we examine the gospels, we see that Jesus repeatedly turns things upside down and leaves people amazed, stunned, enlightened, confused, and sometimes quite angry and upset. To say, for example, blessed are the poor in spirit, blessed are those who mourn, blessed are the meek, and so forth can bring great joy but it can also be quite disturbing.

Jesus sees and names as blessed what many in our culture and ego-driven world would consider completely counterintuitive, lacking in logic and common sense, and downright ludicrous.

How do we, as Jesus' disciples, come to see, value, think, and act as Jesus did? How do we come to *live* the Beatitudes and not just know them intellectually?

A Discerning and Attentive Heart

Like nearly everything in our lives as disciples of Jesus, we must learn the art and discipline of spiritual discernment if we hope to live Christlike lives. The word *discernment* is fairly common in our usage today and generally refers to decision making. Discernment, however, is much more than decision making; it is about developing a discerning heart, a heart that strives to know—as much as anyone could ever know—the mind, heart, and ways of God.

The word *discernment* finds its roots in the Latin word *discernere* and the Greek word *diakrisis*, both of which mean "to separate out, to distinguish, or to sift." We sift or sort out the good from the bad, the inner from the outer, the true from the false, the light from the dark, and even the good from the better, and so forth.

Grounded in prayer, discernment is not limited to decision making, but instead is a daily spiritual practice by which we come to know more fully what is of God and what is not, what leads to living a life more fully in and for God and the Kingdom of God. By living a discerning, reflective life, we come to learn how to live for the greater glory of God.

First and Foremost

A key element in the process of discernment involves being in touch with our desires—and not just any desire but those most intimate desires that often are vocational in nature, penetrating the truth of our being, of who we are as persons.

Good desires are expressions of our true selves, akin to a north star, which can help guide us in the right direction. Desires are bursting with energy and passion, moving us to act, decide, choose, and judge. So in discerning, we ask ourselves: For whom or what do I really long? In the gut of my being, deep in my heart and soul, who do I, if truth be told, yearn to be, and what do I crave to do? For what do I sincerely desire to strive and invest energy in? What is the ultimate gift I want to offer God and the world? Do I desire to live a beatitudinal life and be blessed in the ways that Jesus names a beatitudinal life?

Without a doubt, these are not easy questions to answer. Over the course of our lives, our responses may vary, at least with nuance or degrees of clarity. But the questions and our answers are important because they place us on a path that will lead us to becoming, with the grace of God, what we desire. We will move toward God through what we desire and love.

Deep Listening

Being in touch with our deepest desires as well as the process of discernment as a whole calls for deep listening. Deep listening means that we attend with mind and heart. We listen to the word of God in Scripture, to the voices of the holy men and women present in our rich and ancient Christian tradition. We listen to the Holy Spirit speaking through today's prophets and in the events of daily life.

Also, and in some ways most especially, we listen to the voice within that at times is almost like a gentle whisper. We aspire to develop the habit of this form of listening in an attempt to walk with God in all events, times, and places. Through ongoing discernment, we come to the point when we can say, as did St. Paul: "I live, no longer I, but Christ lives in me" (Galatians 2:20).

As we listen, we will hear the call of God to seek something more— not just any kind of "more," but the more of God and what is of God. In our deep desires to be disciples of Jesus, we will want to understand better what that might mean for us, tangibly. We will want to belong to God more faithfully and be increasingly steadfast in our commitment to God's reign. There will be within us an internal imperative to understand how this can be so in our lives, how our hearts and souls must change for the re-patterning of our inner and outer worlds to come about.

We will be looking for the ways to live on the outside what we are most authentically within! Becoming a beatitudinal person is an act of faithfulness and a blessing for others as well.

> As we listen, we will hear the call of God to seek something more—not just any kind of "more," but the more of God and what is of God.

Growth in Freedom

The Sermon on the Mount, within which we find the Beatitudes, is considered to be a fundamental, essential teaching of Jesus. Here is where the proverbial "rubber hits the road" in discipleship. This is where we must choose to reach out and touch the flame and not just contemplate it.

As we move deeper into this radical life of discipleship, we will experience many different emotions and contradictory thoughts. Likewise, as we set out to become beatitudinal persons, we will discover within ourselves areas of resistance.

Some of the Beatitudes might be easy to relate to and embrace. Others will be more difficult for us to identify with and will reveal some degree of resistance that points to areas of needed reflection and growth—and possibly profound and fundamental conversion as well.

Resistance, in my experience, often points to something that is not free—thus the "push-back." Perhaps there are attachments that must be relinquished because they hold us bound, impeding us from saying yes more fully. So what are we to do? How will we know how to proceed? Again, this is where more ongoing discernment is vital.

As we do the sifting and sorting work of discernment, we grow in self-awareness, which in turn can lead to greater freedom, true freedom in God. We strive to be free from anything that impedes us from living a beatitudinal life. "Freedom from" makes possible "freedom for" and "freedom to" love.

Ultimately, discernment and freedom are about love—love of God and love of others. Like the rich young man in the gospel, we sometimes walk away sad, for the invitation of Jesus calls us to relinquish what we have become attached to. (See Matthew 19:16–22.) As we grow in freedom, we grow in love and, as we grow in love, we grow in freedom.

Fr. Pedro Arrupe (1907-1991), former Superior General of the Jesuits, grew in this love and freedom through his own life of habitual discernment. Toward the end of his life he wrote what has become known as his "Falling in Love Prayer": "Nothing is more practical than finding God, that is, falling in love in a quite absolute final way. What you are in love with, what seizes your imagination, will affect everything. It will decide what will get you out of bed in the morning, what you will do with your evenings, how you will spend your weekends, what you will read, who you know, what breaks your heart, what amazes you with joy and gratitude. Fall in love, stay in love, and it will decide everything."

Examen of Consciousness: A Practical Tool

A helpful tool for ongoing discernment and growing in the beatitudinal life can be found in what is referred to as the "examen of consciousness." This examen, often confused with "examination of conscience" by those who first hear of it, is quite different; it does not primarily seek to know our sins in order, for example, to prepare for the celebration of the Sacrament of Reconciliation.

Rather, this examen seeks to help us become increasingly aware of the spirits that move within us—of the diverse inclinations that are present in our hearts and minds. Thus, by the process of sifting, sorting, and discriminating, we begin to recognize what is of God, the Source of all that is good, and what is not.

The habitual practice of the examen leads to gratitude and joy. And yes, the process also points out areas that are in need of growth or repentance. The primary concern of the examen is the deep reflection that helps us see how we can cooperate more fully with the movement of the

Holy Spirit within us in order to move toward greater trust, love, and faith.

As a result, we are more able to say yes to whatever God asks of us or invites us into. As we practice the examen, we soon learn the truth of the statement of the disciples of Emmaus who reflected on their encounter with Christ: "Were not our hearts burning [within us] while he spoke to us on the way?" (Luke 24:32).

Thus, by the process of sifting, sorting, and discriminating, we begin to recognize what is of God, the Source of all that is good, and what is not.

Examen: Basic Components

This examen of consciousness, which leads to transformed consciousness and more authentic Christian living, has some basic components. Before presenting these elements, let me note that the daily practice of this examen is advisable, and that sufficient time be dedicated to it if we would like this spiritual discipline to bear fruit.

- Begin by entering into quiet, recalling the presence of God and calling upon the guidance of the Holy Spirit.
- Look over the day, noticing the ways in which God was at work. Name the ways you rejoiced and gave thanks.
- Look also for the moments and situations in which you failed to cooperate with the grace of God, when you preferred darkness to light, turned your back on God, gave in to pressure. (Here we also take note of moments of resistance.) Where there is sin, express sorrow. Where there is resistance, ponder its significance.
- Discern what might be needed for tomorrow (if your examen is at the end of your day) or what you need as this day continues to unfold. What grace do you ask of God? What might you need to surrender or change in order to cooperate more fully with God?
- Ask God's blessing and give thanks.

This examen can be a helpful tool in our efforts to live beatitudinal lives. For example, by practicing this examen, we can come to understand what it means to be, as the first Beatitude says, poor in spirit, and how we can daily grow in becoming poor. We can begin to recognize, experientially, how blessed are the poor in spirit for, truly, theirs is the kingdom of heaven.

Conclusion

There is so much more that can be said about discernment and living a beatitudinal life, but the bottom line is found in a comment of the second-century bishop St. Irenaeus who noted that the glory of God is the human person fully alive.

Your Thoughts

1 How do I engage in discernment? What method or process have I applied to date? How has it helped me toward making the right decision toward a healthy and holy life?

_____

_____

_____

2 What do I most desire? How are my desires influencing the decisions I make that enhance or inhibit my ultimate life goals or purpose?

_____

_____

Try This

Study the Scriptures to identify biblical accounts of the struggles and triumphs of discernment in the lives of various biblical characters, like Mary, Joseph, Paul, or the Apostles.

BECOMING *a* BEATITUDE COMMUNITY

SR. ANGELA ANN ZUKOWSKI, MHSH

You sow a thought, you reap an act.
You sow an act, you reap a habit.
You sow a habit, you reap a virtue.
You sow a virtue, you reap a character.
You sow a character, you reap a destiny.
ANONYMOUS

The cultural norms that we see constantly glorified on TV, in movies, in popular music, and on the internet are not making our jobs for creating Beatitude communities (cultures) any easier. The culture that offers so many distractions and temptations to our young people is based on a secular and materialistic view of life that contradicts the core values of the gospel. It is a culture that, at best, is totally indifferent to one's faith life and, at worst, seems to be completely anti-religious and opposed to any yearnings of the spiritual needs of human existence.

Our students will always find paradoxes of the gospel and the culture swirling around them. We are called to nurture within our students a religious experience and language that can prophetically confront modern times. This is the most valued legacy that you and I—as catechists, Catholic educators, and pastoral ministers—can leave to them.

This chapter invites you to accept the challenge to intentionally begin to embrace nurturing a Beatitude community and culture wherever you now stand.

The Role of *Baptizo*

When we gather on a Sunday to celebrate the Eucharist, it is our baptism, in a real sense, that we are celebrating and furthering.

One way the early Greeks used the term *baptizo* (baptism) was in relation to the trade of cloth dying. To change the color of a garment was to place it into boiling dye. To see whether the color had "taken," the cloth had to be lifted out, inspected, and then dipped again into the mixture. The word the Greeks used for repeated dipping into the dye was *baptizo*.

Is this not an appropriate word to describe our journey of faith? We never arrive but are always arriving at a deeper understanding of who Jesus is for us. Daily, we need to experience *baptizo* by living the Beatitudes.

The *Catechism of the Catholic Church* defines virtue as "a habitual and firm disposition to do good" (n. 1833). Traditionally, it is a quality of human character by which individuals habitually recognize and do what is right. A good moral habit is produced of good actions. A habit is not a single action; rather, it is a constant dipping into the dye that makes it work.

Catholic education is more than the acquisition of intellectual values. It is learning a lifestyle in the spirit of the gospels and our Catholic heritage. Catholics have a different worldview that needs to be woven into the full fabric of the faith community: families, neighborhoods, parish, school, and the civic community.

Qualities for Holding the Beatitude Community Together

A sound and solid Beatitude community (culture) can be founded in a clear and comprehensive Pastoral Beatitude Community Plan. It must be woven into every thread (dimension) of the fabric of our faith life.

The term *pastoral* implies the following: personal; compassionate; community sensitive; prophetic; engaging both the mind and heart; and demonstrating an inclusive and rich diversity of dimensions among all those who are influenced by the witness of prophetic discipleship within the countercultural context. There are fundamental qualities or dispositions that hold a Beatitude community together. These qualities must be cultivated through reflective praxis.

These qualities are:

1. the practice of a contemplative (prayerful) stance toward one another, our community, and the world;
2. listening with a sacred—vulnerable and open—heart by being alert, pausing, pondering, and acting with compassion and humility;
3. courage (audacity) to respond to the Beatitudes/Sermon on the Mount within shifting cultural contexts;
4. faithfulness to our call as prophetic disciples grounded in our baptism and confirmation commitments;
5. hope for a "new creation," a new world order rooted in gospel values.

Best Practices for Designing a Pastoral Beatitude Community Plan

The following are select best-practice initiatives that have made a significant difference in establishing catechetical programs and Catholic schools that animate a Beatitude community. You can benefit from their experience.

1. Orchestrate a three-year strategic pastoral plan to enhance the catechetical program's or Catholic school's curriculum for nurturing a Beatitude community throughout the system. Check out "The Tree of Contemplative Practices" (contemplativemind.org/practices/tree.html) for cultivating awareness and developing a stronger connection to God. This can be accomplished by organizing conversations on all parish and

Catholic school levels around depth meaning and potential impact for nurturing a Pastoral Beatitude Community and Faith Formation Plan with faculty and staff.

In some instances, it is helpful to extend the planning process into the parish pastoral council's planning efforts. Incorporate into the plan benchmarks for successful implementation and evaluation.

2. Establish the parameters and grounds for a Beatitude community (culture) that is comprehensive and inclusive of diversity among students, faculty, staff, and environment. This is realized by inviting a support team from the extended faith community to participate in the planning, implementation, and evaluation process. By recognizing the diversity of Beatitude expressions (both religious and cultural), we call for the ownership and commitment among everyone whose life is influenced or touched by our presence within the community.

If working within a Catholic school, establish guidelines for advancing the Beatitude community (culture) throughout the entire curriculum mapping process (refresh all lesson plans). Each year a Beatitude Retreat (faculty, families, and staff) is made available to deepen the community's awareness to the commitment for cultivating a Beatitude community (culture).

3. Collaborate with catechists, faculty, and staff for defining and implementing a Beatitude environment (attitude, aesthetics, art, and special animation) throughout the learning space. A person should be able to walk into our learning environments and sense the Beatitude spirit radiating through both the lived experience and the aesthetic representation.

A successful approach has been promoting a Beatitude Festival of the Arts that integrates various art forms (poetry, music, dance, art, drama, skits, literature, etc.) that helps students express their understanding of a Beatitude way of living.

Invite all parishes and churches within the region to attend and participate in the festival. Encourage local parishes and churches to invite students to display their Beatitude aesthetic exhibits and perform the artistic interpretations produced for the festival. In some instances, local or regional museums may be open to exhibit the students' work in celebration of civic holidays related to justice, peace, and equality.

4. Establish Beatitude Living Recognitions for students, faculty, classrooms, families, and the local community. A special Beatitude Banner, Beatitude Badge, or Beatitude Medal could be awarded each month to the nominated person(s) for endeavoring to prophetically witness to a Beatitude way of life expressed through service-learning or lifestyle.

There is a great diversity as to what is labeled as service-learning. Service-learning should include a balance between service to the community and catechetical formation. It is imperative to realize that the term *community service* (perhaps more commonly referred to as performing "service hours") and the term *service-learning* are not interchangeable terms. Rather, these terms differ markedly in their meaning and how they are implemented.

Performing service hours or community service describes extracurricular activities aimed at doing good for individuals or local institutions. The vast majority of our Catholic schools and/or confirmation programs require students to perform a specified number of service hours.

While the intent of mandating these hours is certainly praiseworthy, the outcome often "dead ends" once the service is performed and the requisite adult "signs off." The responsibility comes to an end when the "hours" are completed. The question remains as to what or how much the student has learned or experienced from performing tasks for service hours.

By focusing on creating a Beatitude community (culture), such experiences are not short-term but long-term. They contribute toward establishing a quality of life and service that is the norm—not the exception.

5. Support of family life is critical for animating a Beatitude community (culture). Invite parents to special morning, early afternoon, or evening reflections on how their households can become Beatitude Family Units in the parish, school, and local community. Such experiences help parents better articulate their role and responsibility. In some instances, you may encourage smaller Beatitude Faith Communities that meet once a month to reflect, pray, and define the procedures for enhancing the parish's and school's Beatitude community (culture).

6. Organize meetings with local pastors and churches to orchestrate the implementation of a comprehensive Beatitude Community Cultural Plan throughout all the neighborhoods. This gathering could reflect on the Beatitudes in light of Catholic social teaching and related ecumenical social justice themes that strive to bring authentic Christian transformation into the entire local setting. Perhaps the parish, school, or local neighborhood community could establish a small endowment primarily focused on nurturing the Beatitude community (culture).

If a transformative difference is to be realized, the entire system (families and neighborhoods) needs to be engaged at all levels. It is a systemic issue and concern.

7. Ensure a robust family Beatitude community (culture) for supporting the implementation of the plan. Invite families within neighborhoods to potluck suppers on the weekend to explore how they can participate in transforming neighborhoods to reflect a Beatitude community (culture). Special T-shirts identifying neighborhoods as select Beatitude communities could become identifying markers. Each year a new Beatitude could be assumed by the neighborhoods to enrich the life of the whole community.

Conclusion

The goal of virtuous living is to become holy, to grow in the image and likeness of God, to develop a loving relationship with Christ, and "to tend toward the good with all one's sensory and spiritual powers" (*Catechism of the Catholic Church*, n. 1803). In an age that shows a decline or obscuring of the moral sense and a rise in subjectivism and utilitarianism, there is a loss of awareness of the marginality of a Beatitude way of living and, with it, an eclipse of fundamental Catholic ethical principles and values.

A depth understanding of the Beatitudes provides a lens for reading our world differently and analytically through the Beatitude lens. The ladder of the Beatitudes is interrelated, interconnected, overlapping. What Jesus says about being poor in spirit has to do with being a peacemaker. Being meek is connected to being merciful. Like a prism, the Beatitudes are ways of living and reflecting the multi-dimensions of God's unconditional love and presence in our lives.

To live the Beatitudes is to be a vessel of God's love by mirroring love into the world, proclaiming the presence and Kingdom of God, and leading all back into the very heart of God—where our journey began.

Your Thoughts

1 What is my experience of popular communications media that seem to contradict the principles and values of a Beatitude community (culture)? (Be specific.)

_____

_____

_____

2 What is the most valued legacy I desire to leave my children or those whom I catechize? (Be specific.)

_____

_____

_____

Try This

Initiate a Beatitude Medal of Honor or a Beatitude Peace Medal to be awarded every month to students for demonstrating outstanding Beatitude living or service learning.

ABOUT THE CONTRIBUTORS

General Editor

Sr. Angela Ann Zukowski, MHSH, DMin, is the Director of the Institute for Pastoral Initiatives (1978–present) and Professor in the Department of Religious Studies of the University of Dayton. She is a member of the Mission Helpers of the Sacred Heart (Towson, MD).

Chapter 1

David Wheeler-Reed is currently a postdoctoral visiting research fellow at Yale Divinity School and an instructor in religious studies at Albertus Magnus College. His work focuses on the New Testament, the ancient family, and gender and sexuality in antiquity.

Chapter 2

Sean Reynolds, PhD, is Director of the Office of Youth and Young Adult Ministry for the Archdiocese of Cincinnati. With more than 35 years experience in catechetical and youth ministry, Sean is a published author and frequent presenter at national gatherings.

Chapter 3

Susan K. Sack earned her doctorate in theology from the University of Dayton. She is a wife, mother of four sons, and longtime teacher, farmer, catechetical leader, and community activist.

Chapter 4

Jane Bensman is experienced in a variety of church ministries. She has served as the Coordinator for Evangelization and Parish Renewal for the Archdiocese of Cincinnati; a Parish Pastoral Associate; a Parish Pastoral Administrator; and Faith Formation Coordinator for Mary Queen of Peace School (Dayton, OH).

Chapter 5

Norm Rich has taught theology for almost 30 years. He is currently teaching at Archbishop Alter High School in Kettering, OH.

Chapter 6

Fr. James Schimelpfening, SM, is in ministry at the University of Dayton where he serves as priest and spiritual director through the Office of Campus Ministry. He teaches a graduate religious studies course in Spiritual Direction and Pastoral Care. Through the years, he has preached numerous retreats and parish missions, and has been on team for directed retreats. As a Marianist, he has lived and ministered in a variety of different settings in Latin America, India, Europe, and North America.

Chapter 7

Sr. Angela Ann Zukowski, MHSH, DMin (See General Editor.)

RECOMMENDED RESOURCES

**The following are available from the
United States Conference of Catholic Bishops
or your local Catholic bookstore**

National Directory for Catechesis. Washington, DC:
United States Conference of Catholic Bishops, 2005

General Directory for Catechesis. Washington, DC. Congregation for
the Clergy. United States Conference of Catholic Bishops, 1997

New American Bible, Revised Edition.
United States Conference of Catholic Bishops, 2011

Catechism of the Catholic Church. Vatican City. Second Edition. 1997

Available online at www.vatican.va

Dogmatic Constitution on Divine Revelation (Dei Verbum)

*The Word of God in the Life and Mission
of the Church (Instrumentum Laboris)*

Dogmatic Constitution on the Church (Lumen Gentium)

Paths of the Church (Ecclesiam Suam)

*Declaration on the Relation of the Church to
Non-Christian Religions (Nostra Aetate)*

Decree on Ecumenism (Unitatis Redintegratio)